PRAYING WITH BEADS

PRAYING WITH BEADS

• • • • •

Daily Prayers
for the Christian Year

Nan Lewis Doerr *&* Virginia Stem Owens

WILLIAM B. EERDMANS PUBLISHING COMPANY
GRAND RAPIDS, MICHIGAN / CAMBRIDGE, U.K.

Published 2007 by
Wm. B. Eerdmans Publishing Co.
2140 Oak Industrial Drive N.E., Grand Rapids, Michigan 49505 /
P.O. Box 163, Cambridge CB3 9PU U.K.
www.eerdmans.com

Printed in the United States of America

12 11 10 09 08 07   7 6 5 4 3 2 1

Library of Congress Cataloging-in-Publication Data

Doerr, Nan Lewis.
Praying with beads: daily prayers for the Christian year /
Nan Lewis Doerr & Virginia Stem Owens.
p.   cm.
ISBN 978-0-8028-2727-2 (pbk.: alk. paper)
1. Church year — Prayers and devotions. 2. Prayers.
I. Owens, Virginia Stem.   II. Title.

BV30.D54   2007
242'.8 — dc22

2007030014

Contents

Introduction

Why Pray with Beads?

Prayer is essential to the Christian life. It is the oxygen of the spirit. The spirit cannot live without this connection to the very source of our being.

Sustaining this connection demands that we attend with mind, body, and soul to this undertaking of prayer. Yet we find it difficult to keep the mind focused for long. The rapid-fire delivery of information by television and the Internet has accustomed us to take in the transmission quickly and move on to the next message demanding our attention. We grow impatient when we have to wait a few extra seconds for a search engine to deliver thousands of links to our queries.

I have found, though, that while electronic communication may be swift, spiritual communion remains a slow process. When I pray, I find it difficult to quiet my mind and decelerate. Yet slowing down is essential to prayer. Indeed, Scripture often admonishes us to "wait upon the Lord."

For an impatient person like me, waiting isn't easy. A dozen inner voices — some anxious, some merely practical — vie for my attention. I think of the perfect comeback in an argument I've had that day or post a mental sticky note to myself to remember a friend's birthday. Or I may construct grocery lists in my mind.

From listening to others who have similar problems praying, I know I am not alone. How are we ever to squelch our mental gibberish and slow ourselves down long enough to enter that place of quietness and peace where we can contemplate eternal truth and renew our trust in God's grace?

Surprisingly, the answer lies in calling on the lowly domain of the physical senses, a realm we might ordinarily think of as opposed to the spiritual. But certain practices that actively involve the body can break our addiction to frenetic speed. The Orthodox tradition, for instance, uses the visual contemplation of icons to focus the attention of the faithful. The monastic practice of chanting psalms aloud necessarily takes more time and effort than reading them silently and keeps the mind from wandering.

As I learned from Nan Doerr, then the assistant rector at my church, prayer beads can serve the same purpose by employing the sense of touch. She taught a group of women who pray regularly for the sick and troubled of our parish how to use the beads to focus and hold our attention.

As our fingers felt first the sharp edges of the cross, then moved on from bead to bead, our brains became more fully engaged in the task of praying. Not only were our minds processing the verbal language of prayer, but we were also absorbing the texture and shape, the heft and size of each bead as it slipped through our fingers. With more parts of the mind fully occupied, there was less occasion for it to wander away from the task literally now at hand. And in praying with beads, we were taking up a practice that was centuries old.

A Brief History of Prayer Beads

The use of prayer beads, though a relatively new practice among Protestants, has a long history in practical spirituality. Probably the most familiar to Western Christians is the praying of the Roman Catholic rosary. However, the use of prayer beads goes back far beyond the Christian era.

The practice probably began over five thousand years ago in

India, where Hindus used pebbles carried in a pouch to count their prayers. This later developed into a string of 108 beads connected with one large bead and a tassel. Buddhists carried over this tradition later with the same number of beads, using them as reminders of the 108 desires that one must overcome in order to achieve Nirvana. Muslims use ninety-nine beads, plus one, to represent the ninety-nine names of God. The extra bead is for the secret name known to Allah alone.

Among Christians, the practice of praying with beads or stones probably originated with the Desert Fathers in the third century. Like the early Hindus, they used pebbles counted out from a leather pouch. Eastern Christians made prayer ropes of knotted wool called "chotki." These chotki were found mostly among monastics, and the number of knots depended on the monastery's tradition. The prayer most often repeated is the Jesus Prayer: "Lord Jesus Christ, have mercy on me, a sinner."

In the Western church, the Irish community of St. Colomba began, around the ninth century, to use knotted strings or beads to count their prayers. Indeed, the modern English word "bead" is derived from the Anglo-Saxon "bede," meaning "prayer."

During the Middle Ages, the practice of praying with beads spread to monasteries throughout Catholic Europe. Originally, 150 beads were used to mark the 150 Psalms, which the monks recited in a cycle each week. When the mostly illiterate laity adopted the practice, a simpler form of prayer had to be substituted for the Psalms. The prayers had to be familiar and easily memorized. At first the Paternoster or "Our Father" (what Protestants know as the Lord's Prayer) was used. Later, when the Ave Maria or "Hail Mary" was added, the beads became known as the rosary, from "rosarium" or "rose garden," because the rose was considered Mary's special flower. The rose was also a Christian symbol for perfection. Though the rosary was widely used by the late Middle Ages, it was not officially sanctioned by the pope until 1520.

During the Reformation, Luther did not abandon the rosary, though he shortened the Ave Maria to this form: "Hail Mary, full of grace. The Lord is with thee. Blessed art thou and the fruit of thy womb, Jesus." In this way he eliminated the plea for Mary to pray for the supplicant. He advised his followers to use the rosary as an aid to meditation.

The more iconoclastic Reformers, including Calvin, forbade the use of prayer beads altogether. They concentrated their attention on scriptural texts and devotional printed matter. They encouraged literacy in order to make the Bible and other approved books accessible to believers. Words, whether written or spoken, predominated. Thus prayer beads, along with other sensory aids to devotion like religious statuary, paintings, and stained-glass windows, were condemned as "popish."

In the Church of England, however, the rosary survived, though its practice faded over the next few centuries. England's Catholic minority continued to support the practice, and some Anglicans today still pray the rosary instead of or in addition to Anglican prayer beads.

Among Christians in America, only Roman Catholics and the various Orthodox congregations kept the practice alive. Then, in the 1980s, an Episcopal priest, the Reverend Lynn Bauman, and a group of parishioners studying contemplative prayer began to explore the age-old custom of praying with beads. They developed the simplified design that uses only thirty-three beads and a cross rather than a crucifix. The prayers themselves relied heavily on Scripture.

The Prayers in This Book

The prayers in this book also rely heavily on Scripture. They were gathered and arranged by Nan Doerr, who has a particular talent for putting together quotations from the Bible and gleanings from the Book of Common Prayer that fit the seasons of the church year — Advent, Christmas, Epiphany, Lent, Easter, and Pentecost.

For the most part, the words of the prayers here are taken from the Scriptures appointed to be read each Sunday in the Episcopal Book of Common Prayer or sometimes from prayers that are part of particular Sunday services. Accordingly, they follow a special order that reinforces the seasons of the church year. The phrasing of the prayers has sometimes been modified to make them more personally meaningful to those who use this book.

The Prayer Beads Pattern

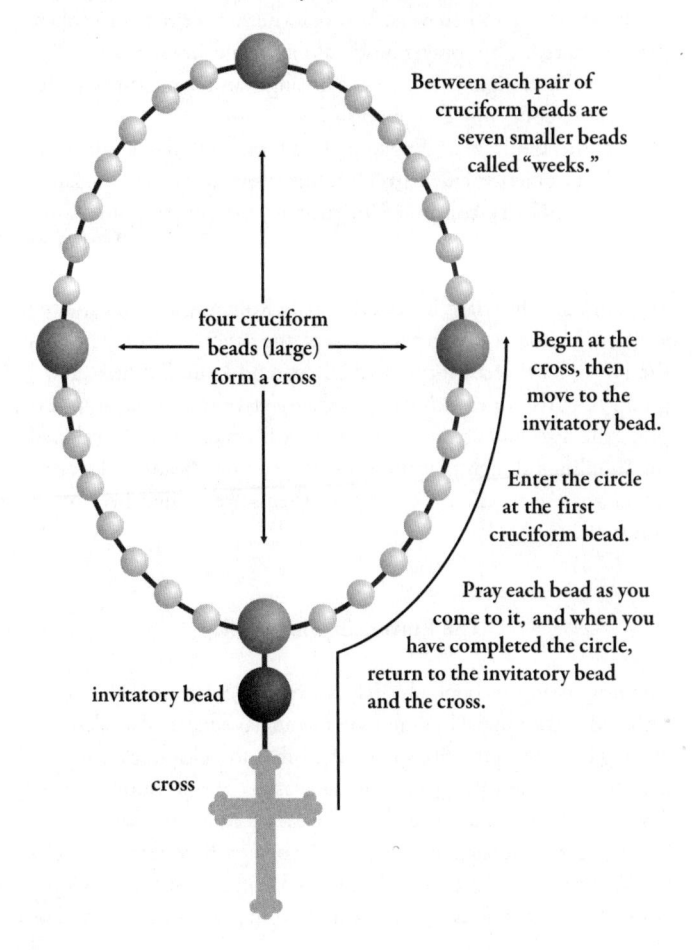

Between each pair of cruciform beads are seven smaller beads called "weeks."

four cruciform beads (large) form a cross

Begin at the cross, then move to the invitatory bead.

Enter the circle at the first cruciform bead.

Pray each bead as you come to it, and when you have completed the circle, return to the invitatory bead and the cross.

invitatory bead

cross

The Anglican prayer beads are composed of a cross and thirty-three beads, five large and twenty-eight small. Thirty-two of the beads form a circle, with one large bead and the cross outside the circle. Inside the circle are four large beads evenly spaced between the twenty-eight smaller beads.

Prayer beads are rich with symbolism. The thirty-three beads remind us of the number of years of Jesus' life on earth before his crucifixion. The four large beads inside the circle are called cruciform beads because they form an invisible cross (see illustration). The small beads divided into groups of seven by the cruciform beads are called "weeks" because they represent the seven days of the week and also recall the seven days of creation. The invitatory bead, the large bead directly above the cross, acts as a call to worship the Lord and invites us into the circle of prayer. And the cross, of course, is replete with symbolism.

In this text, the following visual symbols will be used to represent the components of the prayer beads:

Cross (✝)

Invitatory bead (◉)

Cruciform bead (❖)

Weeks bead (●)

Praying with Beads

When praying with beads, one always starts with the cross. Begin by holding the cross in one hand and acknowledging God's presence. Next, move to the invitatory bead, which is a call to prayer. Then move to the cruciform bead directly above the invitatory bead. On this bead and the three others like it you will usually repeat a verse from Scripture.

Now make your way around the circle, beginning with the first set of seven "weeks" beads. On these beads and on the remaining three sets, you will most often recite the same verse from the Psalms.

When you reach the cruciform bead above the invitatory bead again, repeat the prayer for the cruciform bead a fifth time. When you leave the circle, you will recite the Lord's Prayer on the invitatory bead. When you reach the cross again, you will pray the final prayer, a "sending forth" prayer.

Here's an example of how this "praying around the circle" works — an example that shows you the general pattern of prayer that will be used in this book:

✝ In the name of God, Father, Son, and Holy Spirit. *(Pray while holding the cross.)*

✪ Merciful God, be ever with us, listening to us and strengthening us. *(Pray when you move to the invitatory bead.)*

   ❖ So if you have been raised with Christ, seek the things that are above, where Christ is. *Colossians 3:1 (Pray on each cruciform bead as you reach it.)*

   ● I shall not die, but live, and declare the works of the LORD. *Psalm 118:17 (Pray on each of the "weeks" beads as you move around the circle.)*

✪ The Lord's Prayer *(Pray on the invitatory bead when you leave the circle.)*

✝ Thanks be to God. Amen. *(Pray while holding the cross.)*

Vain Repetitions?

You may be familiar with Jesus' warning about using "vain repetitions" when praying (Matt. 6:7). Consequently, you may feel uneasy repeating the same Scripture verses four times on the cruciform beads and a total of twenty-eight times on the "weeks" beads. Notice, however, that it is *vain,* or useless, repetitions that Jesus cautions against. So the issue is keeping those repetitions from becoming mere meaningless syllables.

The first thing to remember is that God is not impressed by marathon mumbling. But praying with beads in a deliberate and meditative way invites the kind of focused, intentional praying that God honors. The practice of using beads illuminates the fundamental truth that prayer cannot be rushed. It takes time to slow ourselves down enough even to recognize our desire and need to draw close to God.

Similarly, reading and truly absorbing Scripture takes time. No matter how well-intentioned we may be, we tend to skim the passages that are often so familiar to us that we have become indifferent to them. Praying these verses from bead to bead can make us newly aware of their meaning.

Becoming aware of these meanings brings fresh substance and relevance to our prayers. Perhaps a particular verse addresses a particular concern at present. Possibly the words can contain the gratitude one feels for some gift the day has brought. At times I find I can pray a verse on someone else's behalf, using it as an opportunity for intercession. Often I am surprised by the way a prayer guides me into remembering some need of mine or of others, or how it brings to mind a thanksgiving that allows me to savor again God's loving grace.

This is why it is important not to rush through the prayers. They are like nets we let down into the deep waters of our souls in order to draw up parts of our lives that may otherwise go overlooked or disregarded or unpraised. They can break through the barriers of denial and callousness to open broader vistas for the heart and mind.

Using the Prayer Model in This Book

The prayer model in this book offers a simple structure designed for settling the mind and focusing the spirit.

There is a single prayer to be prayed on special days, such as Christmas Eve and Christmas Day, and three prayers for every week of the church year that can be prayed every day of that week. Every three-prayer configuration consists of a morning prayer followed by noon and evening prayers that are variations of the morning prayer.

Remember, though, that this prayer model is meant to be suggestive, not prescriptive. Feel free to tailor it to your own special needs. For example, you might find that one of the three prayers for a given week is most helpful or meaningful to you, and you might want to use it consistently throughout the week. Or you might choose the morning prayer one day and the noon prayer the next. Find the rhythm and pattern for using these prayers that most enriches your prayer life, that allows you to feel God's presence in a deep and tangible way. As you do, remember that the prayer beads provide something to hang onto, a lifeline to the Presence that lies, often hidden or forgotten, at the center of our lives.

Virginia Stem Owens
Holy Week 2007

The Seasons of Advent and Christmas

● ● ● ● ●

A Time of Expectation and Coming

The church year, unlike the calendar year, does not begin on January 1; it starts with the season of Advent. Advent always begins four Sundays before Christmas Day.

Advent means "coming." Note that it is an action in progress, an act not yet accomplished, one we look forward to with renewed hope. Therefore, it is a time of expectation and preparation. It is a time of waiting and watching, of preparing our hearts and minds for the coming of Jesus Christ.

On December 24, the eve of Christmas, Advent ends. The waiting is finally over.

On December 25, the season of Christmas begins. On Christmas Day, the event we have anticipated is finally accomplished: the Incarnation of God in Christ. We revel in the joy that is ours at the birth of our Lord and Savior.

The season of Christmas, which lasts twelve days, highlights special days of remembrance. On December 26 we remember Saint Stephen, the first martyr; on December 27 we remember Saint John the Apostle and Evangelist. On December 28 we remember the innocent children that Herod killed in Bethlehem; and on January 1, New Year's Day, we remember and celebrate Jesus' holy name.

First Week in Advent

Morning Prayer

✝ Our King and Savior now draws near. Come, let us adore him.

☉ Almighty God, give us grace to cast away the works of darkness, and put on the armor of light, that when Jesus comes again in glory, we may rise to eternal life.

> ❖ Come, let us go up to the mountain of the LORD, to the house of the God of Jacob; that he may teach us his ways and that we may walk in his paths. *Isaiah 2:3*

> ● Pray for the peace of Jerusalem: "May they prosper who love you." *Psalm 122:6*

☉ *The Lord's Prayer*

✝ The glory of the Lord shall be revealed, and all flesh shall see it together. Amen.

Noon Variation

> ❖ O LORD, you are our Father; we are the clay, and you are our potter; we are all the work of your hand. *Isaiah 64:8*

> ● Restore us, O God of hosts; show the light of your countenance, and we shall be saved. *Psalm 80:3*

Evening Variation

> ❖ May God our Father and the Lord Jesus Christ make us increase and abound in love for one another and for all. *1 Thessalonians 3:12* (altered)

> ● Offer to God a sacrifice of thanksgiving, and make good your vows to the Most High. *Psalm 50:14*

Second Week in Advent

Morning Prayer

✝ Our King and Savior now draws near. Come, let us adore him.

✪ Merciful God, you sent the prophets to preach repentance and prepare the way for our salvation. Give us grace to heed their warnings and forsake our sins, that we may greet with joy the coming of Jesus our Redeemer.

> ❖ God is able from these stones to raise up children to Abraham. *Matthew 3:9*

> ● Blessed be the Lord GOD, the God of Israel, who alone does wondrous deeds! *Psalm 72:18*

✪ *The Lord's Prayer*

✝ May the God of hope fill us with all joy and peace in believing through the power of the Holy Spirit. Amen.

Noon Variation

> ❖ The Lord is not slow about his promise, as some think of slowness, but is patient with you, not wanting any to perish, but all to come to repentance. *2 Peter 3:9*

> ● Show us your mercy, O LORD, and grant us your salvation. *Psalm 85:7*

Evening Variation

> ❖ I am confident of this, that the one who began a good work among you will bring it to completion by the day of Jesus Christ. *Philippians 1:6*

> ● The LORD has done great things for us, and we are glad indeed. *Psalm 126:4*

Third Week in Advent

Morning Prayer

✝ Our King and Savior now draws near. Come, let us adore him.

☉ Stir up your power, O Lord, and come among us; and because we are hindered by our sins, let your bountiful grace and mercy speedily help and deliver us.

 ❖ The eyes of the blind shall be opened, and the ears of the deaf unstopped; then the lame shall leap like a deer, and the tongue of the speechless sing for joy. *Isaiah 35:5-6*

 ● The LORD sets the prisoners free; the LORD opens the eyes of the blind; the LORD lifts up those who are bowed down. *Psalm 146:7*

☉ *The Lord's Prayer*

✝ May the God of hope fill us with all joy and peace in believing through the power of the Holy Spirit. Amen.

Noon Variation

 ❖ [John said,] "I am the voice of one crying out in the wilderness, 'Make straight the way of the Lord.'" *John 1:23*

 ● When the LORD restored the fortunes of Zion, then were we like those who dream. *Psalm 126:1*

Evening Variation

 ❖ Do not worry about anything, but in everything by prayer and supplication with thanksgiving let your requests be made known to God. *Philippians 4:6*

 ● Surely God is my salvation; I will trust, and will not be afraid. *Isaiah 12:2*

Fourth Week in Advent

Morning Prayer

✝ Our King and Savior now draws near. Come, let us adore him.

✪ Purify our conscience, Almighty God, by your daily visitation, that your Son Jesus Christ, at his coming, may find in us a mansion prepared for himself.

❖ The LORD himself will give you a sign. Look, the young woman is with child and shall bear a son, and shall name him Immanuel. *Isaiah 7:14*

● Those who have clean hands and a pure heart. . . . They shall receive a blessing from the LORD and a just reward from the God of their salvation. *Psalm 24:4-5*

✪ *The Lord's Prayer*

✝ May the God of hope fill us with all joy and peace in believing through the power of the Holy Spirit. Amen.

Noon Variation

❖ Mary said, "Here am I, the servant of the Lord; let it be with me according to your word." *Luke 1:38*

● The LORD has sworn an oath to David . . . : "A son . . . will I set upon your throne." *Psalm 132:11-12*

Evening Variation

❖ When Christ came into the world, he said, "Sacrifices and offerings you have not desired, but a body you have prepared for me. . . . See, God, I have come to do your will, O God." *Hebrews 10:5, 7*

● Restore us, O God of hosts; show the light of your countenance, and we shall be saved. *Psalm 80:3*

Christmas Eve
(December 24)

✝ Alleluia! Unto us a child is born. Come, let us adore him.

☉ O God, who gave this holy night to shine with the true light, grant that we who know him on earth may also enjoy him perfectly in heaven.

   ❖ Blessed is she who believed that there would be a fulfillment of what was spoken to her by the Lord. *Luke 1:45*

   ● My soul magnifies the Lord, and my spirit rejoices in God my Savior. *Luke 1:46*

☉ *The Lord's Prayer*

✝ May the God of hope fill us with all joy and peace in believing through the power of the Holy Spirit. Amen.

Christmas Day
(December 25)

✝ Alleluia! Unto us a child is born. Come, let us adore him.

✪ Almighty God, you have given your only-begotten Son to take our nature upon him, and to be born of a pure virgin; grant that we may daily be renewed by your Holy Spirit.

❖ To you is born this day in the city of David a Savior, who is the Messiah, the Lord. . . . You will find a child wrapped in bands of cloth and lying in a manger. *Luke 2:11-12*

● Sing to the LORD and bless his Name; proclaim the good news of his salvation from day to day. *Psalm 96:2*

✪ *The Lord's Prayer*

✝ May the God of hope fill us with all joy and peace in believing through the power of the Holy Spirit. Amen.

The Remembrance of Saint Stephen
(December 26)

✝ Alleluia! Unto us a child is born. Come, let us adore him.

✿ We give you thanks, O Lord of Glory, for the example of the first martyr Stephen, who prayed for his persecutors.

   ❖ Stephen, full of grace and power, did great wonders and signs among the people. *Acts 6:8*

   ● My times are in your hand; rescue me from the hand of my enemies, and from those who persecute me. *Psalm 31:15*

✿ *The Lord's Prayer*

✝ May the God of hope fill us with all joy and peace in believing through the power of the Holy Spirit. Amen.

The Remembrance of Saint John
(December 27)

✝ Alleluia! Unto us a child is born. Come, let us adore him.

☉ Shed upon your Church, O Lord, the brightness of your light, that we may so walk in the light of your truth.

❖ We declare to you what was from the beginning, what we have heard, what we have seen with our eyes, what we have looked at and touched with our hands, concerning the word of life. *1 John 1:1-2*

● It is a good thing to give thanks to the LORD, and to sing praises to your Name, O Most High. *Psalm 92:1*

☉ *The Lord's Prayer*

✝ May the God of hope fill us with all joy and peace in believing through the power of the Holy Spirit. Amen.

The Remembrance of the Holy Innocents
(December 28)

✝ Alleluia! Unto us a child is born. Come, let us adore him.

⊙ We remember today the slaughter of the holy innocents of Bethlehem by King Herod. Receive into the arms of your mercy all innocent victims and frustrate the designs of evil.

❖ A voice was heard in Ramah, . . . Rachel weeping for her children; she refused to be consoled, because they are no more. *Matthew 2:18*

● Our help is in the Name of the LORD, the maker of heaven and earth. *Psalm 124:8*

⊙ *The Lord's Prayer*

✝ May the God of hope fill us with all joy and peace in believing through the power of the Holy Spirit. Amen.

First Sunday after Christmas

Morning Prayer

✝ Alleluia! Unto us a child is born. Come, let us adore him.

✪ Almighty God, you poured upon us the new light of your incarnate Word; grant that this light, enkindled in our hearts, may shine forth in our lives. Amen.

❖ I will greatly rejoice in the LORD, . . . for he has clothed me with the garments of salvation. *Isaiah 61:10*

● Great is our LORD and mighty in power; there is no limit to his wisdom. *Psalm 147:5*

✪ *The Lord's Prayer*

✝ May the God of hope fill us with all joy and peace in believing through the power of the Holy Spirit. Amen.

Noon Variation

❖ In the beginning was the Word, and the Word was with God, and the Word was God. *John 1:1*

● [The LORD] sends out his command to the earth, and his word runs very swiftly. *Psalm 147:16*

Evening Variation

❖ He was in the world, and the world came into being through him; yet the world did not know him. *John 1:10*

● The LORD has pleasure in those who fear him, in those who await his gracious favor. *Psalm 147:12*

The Remembrance of the Holy Name of Jesus
(January 1)

✝ In the Name of God, Father, Son, and Holy Spirit. Amen.

✪ Almighty God, you poured upon us the new light of your Word made flesh; grant that this light, enkindled in our hearts, may shine forth in our lives. Amen.

❖ After eight days had passed, it was time to circumcise the child; and he was called Jesus, the name given by the angel. *Luke 2:21*

● O LORD our Governor, how exalted is your Name in all the world! *Psalm 8:1*

✪ *The Lord's Prayer*

✝ May the God of hope fill us with all joy and peace in believing through the power of the Holy Spirit. Amen.

Second Sunday after Christmas

Morning Prayer

✝ Behold, the dwelling of God is with humankind. He will dwell with them and be their God.

✪ O God, you created and restored the dignity of human nature; grant that we may share the divine life of him who humbled himself to share our humanity. Amen.

❖ I will lead them back, I will let them walk by brooks of water, in a straight path in which they shall not stumble. *Jeremiah 31:9*

● No good thing will the LORD withhold from those who walk with integrity. *Psalm 84:11*

✪ *The Lord's Prayer*

✝ May the God of hope fill us with all joy and peace in believing through the power of the Holy Spirit. Amen.

Noon Variation

❖ I will turn their mourning into joy; I will comfort them, and give them gladness for sorrow. *Jeremiah 31:13*

● Happy are the people whose strength is in you, whose hearts are set on the pilgrims' way. *Psalm 84:4*

Evening Variation

❖ They found him in the temple, sitting among the teachers, listening to them and asking them questions. And all who heard him were amazed. *Luke 2:46-47*

● Happy are they who dwell in your house! They will always be praising you. *Psalm 84:3*

The Season of Epiphany

● ● ● ● ●

A Time of Light and Revelation

Following the twelfth day of Christmas, the season of Epiphany begins. It always starts on January 6 and ends with the Tuesday before Ash Wednesday.

The word *Epiphany* means "the revealing" or "the showing forth." The Scriptures used during this season, beginning with the passage about the three wise men, focus on the recognition of Jesus as the Son of God. These Scriptures extend that theme to include the recognition of Christ in our own lives and in the image of God that dwells in all people.

The season also focuses on growth — the growth and flowering of Christ's ministry in Galilee. The season ends with lessons on the Transfiguration, which dramatically underscored Jesus' identity as the Messiah.

January 6
(Epiphany)

✝ Nations shall come to your light, and kings to the brightness of your rising.

✪ O God, by a star you led the magi to your only Son; guide us who know you by faith, to your presence where we may see your glory face to face.

   ❖ God shows no partiality, but in every nation anyone who fears him and does what is right is acceptable to him. *Acts 10:34-35*

   ● All kings shall bow down before him, and all the nations do him service. *Psalm 72:11*

✪ *The Lord's Prayer*

✝ May the God of hope fill us with all joy and peace in believing through the power of the Holy Spirit. Amen.

First Week after Epiphany
(Sunday after January 6)

Morning Prayer

✝ Nations shall come to your light, and kings to the brightness of your rising.

✪ Father in heaven, who at the baptism of Jesus proclaimed him your beloved Son: Grant that all who are baptized into his Name may boldly confess him as Lord and Savior. Amen.

   ❖ When Jesus had been baptized, . . . the heavens were opened to him and he saw the Spirit of God descending like a dove. *Matthew 3:16*

   ● The heavens bear witness to your wonders, O LORD, and to your faithfulness in the assembly of the holy ones. *Psalm 89:5*

✪ *The Lord's Prayer*

✝ The glory of the Lord has been revealed, and all flesh shall see it together. Amen.

Noon Variation

   ❖ [John proclaimed], "The one who is more powerful than I is coming. . . . I have baptized you with water; but he will baptize you with the Holy Spirit." *Mark 1:7-8*

   ● Who in the skies can be compared to the LORD? Who is like the LORD among the gods? *Psalm 89:6*

Evening Variation

   ❖ God anointed Jesus of Nazareth with the Holy Spirit and with power; [and] he went about doing good and healing all who were oppressed. *Acts 10:38*

   ● Yours are the heavens; the earth also is yours; you laid the foundations of the world and all that is in it. *Psalm 89:11*

Second Week after Epiphany

Morning Prayer

✝ Nations shall come to your light, and kings to the brightness of your rising.

☸ Almighty God, whose Son Jesus is the light of the world: Grant that your people may so shine with the radiance of Christ's glory that he may be known, worshiped, and obeyed to the ends of the earth. Amen.

❖ [John said,] "Here is the Lamb of God. . . . I saw the Spirit descending from heaven like a dove, and it remained on him." *John 1:29, 32*

● Happy are they who trust in the LORD! They do not resort to evil spirits or turn to false gods. *Psalm 40:4*

☸ *The Lord's Prayer*

✝ The glory of the Lord has been revealed, and all flesh shall see it together. Amen.

Noon Variation

❖ The LORD called me before I was born; while I was in my mother's womb he named me. *Isaiah 49:1*

● Your loving-kindness is better than life itself; my lips shall give you praise. *Psalm 63:3*

Evening Variation

❖ I want you to understand that . . . no one can say "Jesus is Lord" except by the Holy Spirit. *1 Corinthians 12:3*

● I [will] remember you upon my bed, and meditate on you in the night watches. *Psalm 63:6*

Third Week after Epiphany

Morning Prayer

✝ Nations shall come to your light, and kings to the brightness of your rising.

✪ Give us grace, O Lord, to answer the call of Jesus and proclaim the Good News of his salvation, that the whole world may perceive the glory of his marvelous works. Amen.

> ❖ [Jesus said,] "The Spirit of the Lord is upon me, because he has anointed me to bring good news to the poor." *Luke 4:18*

> ● He takes up the weak out of the dust and lifts up the poor from the ashes. *Psalm 113:6*

✪ *The Lord's Prayer*

✝ The glory of the Lord has been revealed, and all flesh shall see it together. Amen.

Noon Variation

> ❖ Ezra brought the law. . . . He read from it . . . from early morning until midday, in the presence of the men and the women and those who could understand. *Nehemiah 8:2-4*

> ● Let the Name of the LORD be blessed, from this time forth for evermore. *Psalm 113:2*

Evening Variation

> ❖ The time is fulfilled, and the kingdom of God has come near; repent, and believe in the good news. *Mark 1:15*

> ● I wait for the LORD; my soul waits for him; in his word is my hope. *Psalm 130:4*

Fourth Week after Epiphany

Morning Prayer

✝ Nations shall come to your light, and kings to the brightness of your rising.

✪ Everlasting God, you govern all things in heaven and on earth; mercifully hear the prayers of your people, and in our time grant us your peace. Amen.

❖ Blessed are those who hunger and thirst for righteousness, for they will be filled. *Matthew 5:6*

● Put your trust in the LORD and do good; dwell in the land and feed on its riches. *Psalm 37:3*

✪ *The Lord's Prayer*

✝ The glory of the Lord has been revealed, and all flesh shall see it together. Amen.

Noon Variation

❖ Since you are eager for spiritual gifts, strive to excel in them for building up the church. *1 Corinthians 14:12*

● You are my hope, O LORD GOD, my confidence since I was young. *Psalm 71:5*

Evening Variation

❖ The LORD your God will raise up for you a prophet . . . from among your own people. *Deuteronomy 18:15*

● He makes his marvelous works to be remembered; the LORD is gracious and full of compassion. *Psalm 111:4*

Fifth Week after Epiphany

Morning Prayer

✝ Nations shall come to your light, and kings to the brightness of your rising.

✪ Set us free, O God, from the bondage of our sins, and give us the liberty of that abundant life which you have made known in your Son our Savior Jesus Christ. Amen.

> ❖ In the morning, while it was still very dark, [Jesus] got up and went out to a deserted place, and there he prayed. *Mark 1:35*

> ● I cry to the LORD with my voice; to the LORD I make loud supplication. *Psalm 142:1*

✪ *The Lord's Prayer*

✝ The glory of the Lord has been revealed, and all flesh shall see it together. Amen.

Noon Variation

> ❖ Let your light shine before others, so that they may see your good works and give glory to your Father in heaven. *Matthew 5:16*

> ● Show me your way, O LORD; lead me on a level path. *Psalm 27:15*

Evening Variation

> ❖ I stand in awe, O LORD, of your work. In our own time revive it; in our own time make it known. *Habakkuk 3:2*

> ● One thing I seek; that I may dwell in the house of the LORD all the days of my life. *Psalm 27:5*

Sixth Week after Epiphany

Morning Prayer

✝ Nations shall come to your light, and kings to the brightness of your rising.

✿ O God, the strength of all who trust in you: accept our prayers and give us your grace, that in keeping your commandments we may please you both in will and deed. Amen.

❖ If you choose, you can keep the commandments, and to act faithfully is a matter of your own choice. *Ecclesiasticus 15:15*

● With my whole heart I seek you; let me not stray from your commandments. *Psalm 119:10*

✿ *The Lord's Prayer*

✝ The glory of the Lord has been revealed, and all flesh shall see it together. Amen.

Noon Variation

❖ The one who plants and the one who waters have a common purpose. . . . For we are God's servants, working together. *1 Corinthians 3:8-9*

● I will meditate on your commandments and give attention to your ways. *Psalm 119:15*

Evening Variation

❖ I the LORD test the mind and search the heart, to give to all according to their ways, according to the fruit of their doings. *Jeremiah 17:10*

● As the deer longs for the water-brooks, so longs my soul for you, O God. *Psalm 42:1*

Seventh Week after Epiphany

Morning Prayer

✝ Nations shall come to your light, and kings to the brightness of your rising.

☉ O God, you have taught us that without love, whatever we do is worth nothing: Send your Holy Spirit and pour into our hearts your greatest gift, which is love, the true bond of peace and of all virtue. Amen.

❖ Do you not know that you are God's temple and that God's Spirit dwells in you? *1 Corinthians 3:16*

● O God, be not far from me; come quickly to help me, O my God. *Psalm 71:12*

☉ *The Lord's Prayer*

✝ The glory of the Lord has been revealed, and all flesh shall see it together. Amen.

Noon Variation

❖ I am about to do a new thing; now it springs forth, do you not perceive it? *Isaiah 43:19*

● Commit your way to the LORD and put your trust in him, and he will bring it to pass. *Psalm 37:5*

Evening Variation

❖ Just as we have borne the image of the man of dust, we will also bear the image of the man of heaven. *1 Corinthians 15:49*

● Be still before the LORD and wait patiently for him. *Psalm 37:7*

Eighth Week after Epiphany

Morning Prayer

✝ Nations shall come to your light, and kings to the brightness of your rising.

✪ Most loving Father, preserve us from faithless fears and worldly anxieties, that nothing in this life may hide from us the light of love that is immortal in your Son, Jesus Christ. Amen.

  ❖ The LORD has comforted his people, and will have compassion on his suffering ones. *Isaiah 49:13b*

  ● For God alone my soul in silence waits; truly, my hope is in him. *Psalm 62:6*

✪ *The Lord's Prayer*

✝ The glory of the Lord has been revealed, and all flesh shall see it together. Amen.

Noon Variation

  ❖ Consider the lilies of the field, how they grow . . . even Solomon in all his glory was not clothed like one of these. *Matthew 6:28-29*

  ● In God is my safety and my honor; God is my strong rock and my refuge. *Psalm 62:8*

Evening Variation

  ❖ [Those who heed my word are] like a man building a house, who dug deeply and laid the foundation on rock; when a flood arose, the river burst against that house but could not shake it. *Luke 6:47-48*

  ● Those who are planted in the house of the LORD shall flourish in the courts of our God. *Psalm 92:12*

Last Week after Epiphany

Morning Prayer

✝ Nations shall come to your light, and kings to the brightness of your rising.

✪ O God, who revealed your Son in glory on the mountain, grant that we, beholding by faith the light of his countenance, may be strengthened to bear our cross, and be changed into his likeness. Amen.

> ❖ I want to know Christ and the power of his resurrection and the sharing of his sufferings by becoming like him in his death. *Philippians 3:10*

> ● Proclaim the greatness of the LORD our God and worship him upon his holy hill. *Psalm 99:9*

✪ *The Lord's Prayer*

✝ The glory of the Lord has been revealed, and all flesh shall see it together. Amen.

Noon Variation

> ❖ When Elijah heard [the sound of sheer silence], he wrapped his face in his mantle and went out and stood at the entrance of the cave. *1 Kings 19:13*

> ● You speak in my heart and say, "Seek my face." Your face, LORD, will I seek. *Psalm 27:11*

Evening Variation

> ❖ We had been eyewitnesses of his majesty. . . . We ourselves heard this voice come from heaven, while we were with him on the holy mountain. *2 Peter 1:16, 18*

> ● One thing I seek; . . . To behold the fair beauty of the LORD and to seek him in his temple. *Psalm 27:5-6*

The Season of Lent

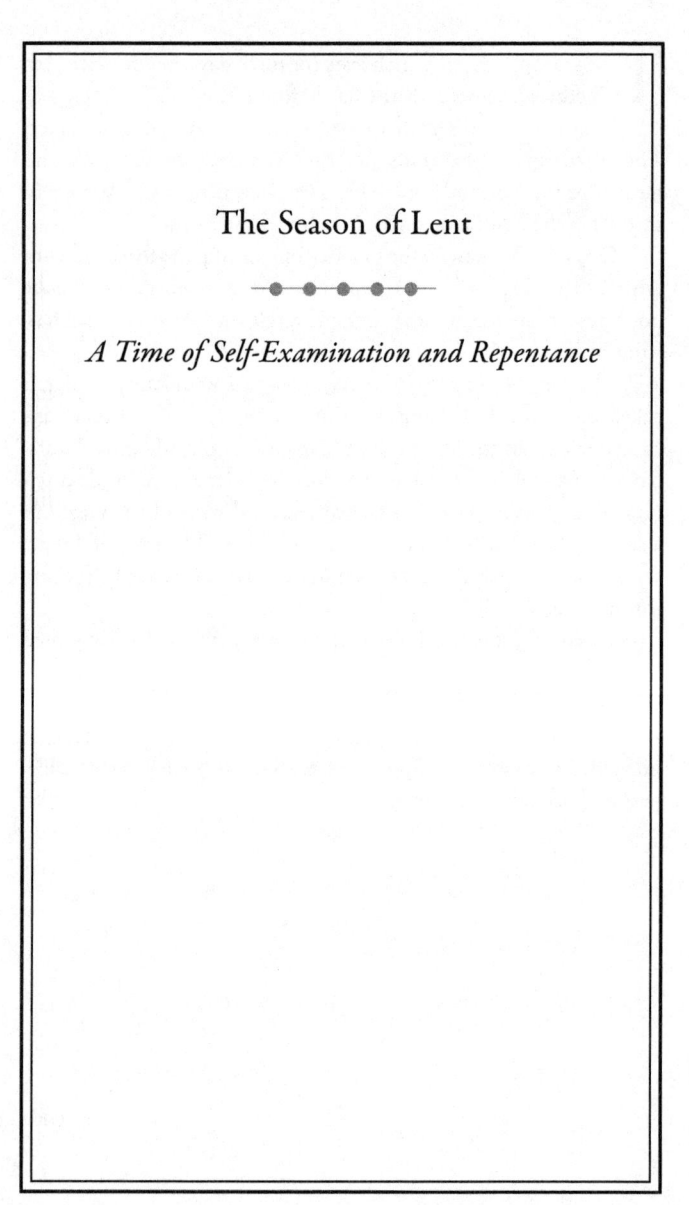

A Time of Self-Examination and Repentance

The season of Lent, which lasts for forty days, begins with Ash Wednesday and ends the day before Easter.

This time is used for self-examination and repentance. The word *repentance* translates the Greek word *metanoia* and means "to turn around" or "to head in a new direction." We are to throw off the mantle of sin and return to the Lord.

On Ash Wednesday the practice of marking the forehead with ashes in the shape of a cross reminds us of our mortality. We are powerless in the face of death and must rely on Christ to redeem us from futility.

The week leading up to Easter, beginning with Palm Sunday, is called Holy Week. During this time we remember and mark the special events in the last week of Christ's life. On Maundy Thursday we remember the last supper that Jesus shared with his disciples. The focus is not only on the bread and wine of the meal but also on Jesus' washing of his disciples' feet. This act of loving servanthood established the standard that was to guide them throughout their lives.

Good Friday is the day on which we remember that Jesus died on the cross. We remember that Jesus gave his life for our sins, and we celebrate his obedience even unto death. On Holy Saturday Jesus lay in the grave. This is a dark day that seemed to be without hope. But Jesus' resurrection on Easter Sunday banished that darkness and renewed our hope.

Ash Wednesday

✝ The Lord is full of compassion and mercy. Come, let us adore him.

✪ Almighty God, you forgive the sins of all who are penitent. Create in us new and contrite hearts, that we may obtain from you, perfect forgiveness of our sins. Amen.

  ❖ Rend your hearts and not your clothing. Return to the LORD, your God, for he is gracious and merciful, slow to anger, and abounding in steadfast love. *Joel 2:13*

  ● As a father cares for his children, so does the LORD care for those who fear him. *Psalm 103:13*

✪ *The Lord's Prayer*

✝ May God grant us forgiveness of sins as we forgive others. Amen.

First Week in Lent

Morning Prayer

✝ The Lord is full of compassion and mercy. Come, let us adore him.

✪ Almighty God, whose blessed Son was led by the Spirit to be tempted by Satan: Come quickly to help us who are assaulted by temptations; and as you know our weakness, save us, O Lord, by your mighty power. Amen.

❖ Just as one man's trespass led to condemnation for all, so one man's act of righteousness leads to justification and life for all. *Romans 5:18*

● Create in me a clean heart, O God, and renew a right spirit within me. *Psalm 51:11*

✪ *The Lord's Prayer*

✝ May God grant us forgiveness of sins as we forgive others. Amen.

Noon Variation

❖ I have set my bow in the clouds, and it shall be a sign of the covenant between me and the earth. *Genesis 9:13*

● Remember, O LORD, your compassion and love, for they are from everlasting. *Psalm 25:5*

Evening Variation

❖ If you confess with your lips that Jesus is Lord and believe in your heart that God raised him from the dead, you will be saved. *Romans 10:9*

● He shall give his angels charge over you, to keep you in all your ways. *Psalm 91:11*

Second Week in Lent

Morning Prayer

✝ The Lord is full of compassion and mercy. Come, let us adore him.

✪ O God, be gracious to all who have gone astray from your ways, and bring them again with penitent hearts and steadfast faith to embrace and hold fast your unchanging truth. Amen.

❖ God did not send the Son into the world to condemn the world, but in order that the world might be saved through him. *John 3:17*

● Our soul waits for the LORD; he is our help and our shield. *Psalm 33:20*

✪ *The Lord's Prayer*

✝ May God grant us forgiveness of sins as we forgive others. Amen.

Noon Variation

❖ It is Christ Jesus, who died, yes, who was raised, who is at the right hand of God, who indeed intercedes for us. *Romans 8:34*

● I have set the LORD always before me; because he is at my right hand I shall not fall. *Psalm 16:8*

Evening Variation

❖ How often have I desired to gather your children together as a hen gathers her brood under her wings. *Luke 13:34*

● Though my father and my mother forsake me, the LORD will sustain me. *Psalm 27:14*

Third Week in Lent

Morning Prayer

✝ The Lord is full of compassion and mercy. Come, let us adore him.

✪ Almighty God, keep our bodies and souls so that we may be defended from all adversities and evil thoughts, that we may live and reign with you. Amen.

    ❖ God is spirit, and those who worship him must worship in spirit and truth. *John 4:24*

    ● Come, let us bow down, and bend the knee, and kneel before the LORD our Maker. *Psalm 95:6*

✪ *The Lord's Prayer*

✝ May God grant us forgiveness of sins as we forgive others. Amen.

Noon Variation

    ❖ Six days you shall labor and . . . work. But the seventh day is a Sabbath to the LORD your God. *Exodus 20:9-10a*

    ● Let the words of my mouth and the meditation of my heart be acceptable in your sight, O LORD. *Psalm 19:14*

Evening Variation

    ❖ Remove the sandals from your feet, for the place on which you are standing is holy ground. *Exodus 3:5*

    ● The LORD has set his throne in heaven, and his kingship has dominion over all. *Psalm 103:19*

Fourth Week in Lent

Morning Prayer

✝ The Lord is full of compassion and mercy. Come, let us adore him.

✪ Gracious Father, whose blessed Son came down from heaven to be bread for the world and give us true life; give us this bread that he may live in us and we in him. Amen.

❖ The LORD does not see as mortals see; they look on the outward appearance, but the LORD looks on the heart. *1 Samuel 16:7b*

● You spread a table before me in the presence of those who trouble me. *Psalm 23:5a*

✪ *The Lord's Prayer*

✝ May God grant us forgiveness of sins as we forgive others. Amen.

Noon Variation

❖ We are what [God] has made us, created in Christ Jesus for good works. *Ephesians 2:10*

● I was glad when they said to me, "Let us go to the house of the LORD." *Psalm 122:1*

Evening Variation

❖ So if anyone is in Christ, there is a new creation: everything old has passed away; see, everything has become new! *2 Corinthians 5:17*

● Taste and see that the LORD is good; happy are they who trust in him! *Psalm 34:8*

Fifth Week in Lent

Morning Prayer

✝ The Lord is full of compassion and mercy. Come, let us adore him.

✪ Almighty God, you alone bring order into the world. Grant us grace to love what you command and desire what you promise that our hearts may be fixed on doing your will. Amen.

❖ I will put my spirit within you, and you shall live, and . . . you shall know that I, the LORD, have spoken and will act. *Ezekiel 37:14*

● O Israel, wait for the LORD, for with the LORD there is mercy. *Psalm 130:6*

✪ *The Lord's Prayer*

✝ May God grant us forgiveness of sins as we forgive others. Amen.

Noon Variation

❖ Unless a grain of wheat falls into the earth and dies, it remains just a single grain; but if it dies, it bears much fruit. *John 12:24*

● Cast me not away from your presence, and take not your holy Spirit from me. *Psalm 51:12*

Evening Variation

❖ Do not remember the former things, or consider the things of old. I am about to do a new thing. *Isaiah 43:18-19a*

● The LORD has done great things for us, and we are glad indeed. *Psalm 126:4*

Holy Week in Lent: Palm Sunday

✝ The Lord is full of compassion and mercy. Come, let us adore him.

☉ Almighty God, whose most dear Son suffered pain and death before he entered into glory, grant that we, walking in the way of the cross, may find it the way of life and peace. Amen.

❖ Let the same mind be in you that was in Christ Jesus, who, though he was in the form of God, did not regard equality with God as something to be exploited, but emptied himself . . . being born in human likeness. *Philippians 2:5-7*

● Our forefathers put their trust in you; they trusted, and you delivered them. *Psalm 22:4*

☉ *The Lord's Prayer*

✝ May God grant us forgiveness of sins as we forgive others. Amen.

Holy Week in Lent: Maundy Thursday

✝ The Lord is full of compassion and mercy. Come, let us adore him.

☉ Almighty Father, whose most dear Son, on the night before he died, instituted the Sacrament of his Body and Blood; who suffered pain and death before he entered into glory, grant that we, walking in the way of the cross, may find it the way of life and peace.

❖ Do you know what I have done to you? . . . I have set you an example, that you also should do as I have done to you. *John 13:12b, 15*

● So mortals ate the bread of angels; he provided for them food enough. *Psalm 78:25*

☉ *The Lord's Prayer*

✝ May God grant us forgiveness of sins as we forgive others. Amen.

Holy Week in Lent: Good Friday

✝ The Lord is full of compassion and mercy. Come, let us adore him.

✪ Almighty God, graciously behold your family for whom our Lord Jesus was willing to suffer death upon the cross. Amen.

❖ But he was wounded for our transgressions, crushed for our iniquities; upon him was the punishment that made us whole, and by his bruises we are healed. *Isaiah 53:5*

● Yet you are the Holy One, enthroned upon the praises of Israel. *Psalm 22:3*

✪ *The Lord's Prayer*

✝ May God grant us forgiveness of sins as we forgive others. Amen.

Holy Week in Lent: Holy Saturday

✝ The Lord is full of compassion and mercy. Come, let us adore him.

✪ Almighty God, whose most dear Son suffered pain and death before he entered into glory, grant that we, walking in the way of the cross, may find it the way of life and peace.

❖ So Joseph took the body and wrapped it in a clean linen cloth and laid it in his own new tomb. *Matthew 27:59-60a*

● But as for me, I have trusted in you, O LORD. I have said, "You are my God." *Psalm 31:14*

✪ *The Lord's Prayer*

✝ May God grant us forgiveness of sins as we forgive others. Amen.

The Season of Easter

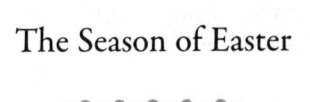

A Time of Resurrection and New Life

Like the Christmas season, the Easter season is a time to celebrate the accomplishment of God's purpose on earth. Specifically, the Easter season is a time of resurrection and new life.

Easter is a time of rejoicing in Jesus' victory over death. Jesus' resurrection confirms that Satan and sin have no final hold over us, and reassures us that in Jesus Christ we have the promise of eternal life.

During this season we celebrate the Lord's continuing presence with us on this earth. We know that Christ has promised to be with us through the Holy Spirit and available to us through prayer.

During this season we also celebrate two special days. The ascension of Jesus took place forty days after Easter. On Ascension Day we remember the apostles standing on the hillside, watching as Jesus rose up into heaven to return to God the Father.

Pentecost comes fifty days after Easter. On this day we remember the Holy Spirit coming down and inspiring and empowering the apostles to go out and spread the gospel to all nations.

Week Beginning with Easter Day

Morning Prayer

✝ Alleluia! Christ is risen. The Lord is risen indeed. Alleluia!

✪ Almighty God, grant that we who celebrate with joy the day of the Lord's resurrection may be raised from the death of sin by your life-giving Spirit. Amen.

❖ Why do you look for the living among the dead? He is not here, but has risen. *Luke 24:5b*

● On this day the LORD has acted; we will rejoice and be glad in it. *Psalm 118:24*

✪ *The Lord's Prayer*

✝ Thanks be to God, who gives us victory over death through Jesus our Lord. Amen.

Noon Variation

❖ If you have been raised with Christ, seek the things that are above, where Christ is, seated at the right hand of God. *Colossians 3:1*

● I will give thanks to you, for you answered me and have become my salvation. *Psalm 118:21*

Evening Variation

❖ We know that Christ, being raised from the dead, will never die again; death no longer has dominion over him. *Romans 6:9*

● This is the LORD's doing, and it is marvelous in our eyes. *Psalm 118:23*

Second Week in Easter

Morning Prayer

✝ Alleluia! Christ is risen. The Lord is risen indeed. Alleluia!

✿ Everlasting God, you established the new covenant of reconciliation; grant that we who are reborn into the fellowship of Christ's body may show forth in our lives what we profess by our faith. Amen.

❖ Blessed are those who have not seen and yet have come to believe. *John 20:29b*

● This is the gate of the LORD; he who is righteous may enter. *Psalm 118:20*

✿ *The Lord's Prayer*

✝ Thanks be to God, who gives us victory over death through Jesus our Lord. Amen.

Noon Variation

❖ The love of God is this, that we obey his commandments. And his commandments are not burdensome. *1 John 5:3*

● I will give thanks to the LORD with my whole heart, in the assembly of the upright, in the congregation. *Psalm 111:1*

Evening Variation

❖ I know that you can do all things, and that no purpose of yours can be thwarted. *Job 42:2*

● Great are the deeds of the LORD! They are studied by all who delight in them. *Psalm 111:2*

Third Week in Easter

Morning Prayer

✝ Alleluia! Christ is risen. The Lord is risen indeed. Alleluia!

☉ O God, open the eyes of our faith, that we may behold Christ in all his redeeming work. Amen.

❖ Were not our hearts burning within us while he was talking to us on the road, while he was opening the scriptures to us? *Luke 24:32*

● I will walk in the presence of the LORD, in the land of the living. *Psalm 116:8*

☉ *The Lord's Prayer*

✝ Thanks be to God, who gives us victory over death through Jesus our Lord. Amen.

Noon Variation

❖ Come, let us go up to the mountain of the LORD, to the house of the God of Jacob; that he may teach us his ways and that we may walk in his paths. *Micah 4:2*

● Sing to the LORD a new song, for he has done marvelous things. *Psalm 98:1*

Evening Variation

❖ [The Lord said of Saul,] "He is an instrument whom I have chosen to bring my name before Gentiles and kings and before the people of Israel." *Acts 9:15*

● The word of the LORD is right, and all his works are sure. *Psalm 33:4*

Fourth Week in Easter

Morning Prayer

✝ Alleluia! Christ is risen. The Lord is risen indeed. Alleluia!

☉ O God, whose son is the good shepherd, grant that when we hear his voice we may know him and follow where he leads. Amen.

❖ He himself bore our sins in his body on the cross, so that, free from sins, we might live for righteousness. *1 Peter 2:24*

● The LORD is my shepherd; I shall not be in want. *Psalm 23:1*

☉ *The Lord's Prayer*

✝ Thanks be to God, who gives us victory over death through Jesus our Lord. Amen.

Noon Variation

❖ See what love the Father has given us, that we should be called children of God; and that is what we are. *1 John 3:1*

● Know this: The LORD himself is God; he himself has made us, and we are his. *Psalm 100:2a*

Evening Variation

❖ My sheep hear my voice. I know them, and they follow me. I give them eternal life, and they will never perish. *John 10:27-28*

● Though I walk through the valley of the shadow of death, I shall fear no evil; for you are with me; your rod and your staff, they comfort me. *Psalm 23:4*

Fifth Week in Easter

Morning Prayer

✝ Alleluia! Christ is risen. The Lord is risen indeed. Alleluia!

✪ Almighty God, grant that we know Jesus so perfectly to be the way, the truth, and the life that we may steadfastly follow his steps in the way that leads to eternal life. Amen.

 ❖ You are a chosen race, a royal priesthood, a holy nation, God's own people, in order that you may proclaim the mighty acts of him who called you out of darkness into his marvelous light. *1 Peter 2:9*

 ● Come now and see the works of God, how wonderful he is in his doing toward all people. *Psalm 66:4*

✪ *The Lord's Prayer*

✝ Thanks be to God, who gives us victory over death through Jesus our Lord. Amen.

Noon Variation

 ❖ If our hearts do not condemn us, we have boldness before God; and we receive from him whatever we ask, because we obey his commandments and do what pleases him. *1 John 3:21-22*

 ● Bless our God, you peoples; make the voice of his praise to be heard. *Psalm 66:7*

Evening Variation

 ❖ I give you a new commandment, that you love one another. Just as I have loved you. . . . By this everyone will know that you are my disciples. *John 13:34-35*

 ● The LORD is faithful in all his words and merciful in all his deeds. *Psalm 145:14*

Sixth Week in Easter

Morning Prayer

✝ Alleluia! Christ is risen. The Lord is risen indeed. Alleluia!

✪ O God, pour into our hearts such love toward you that we, loving you above all things, may obtain your promises, which exceed all that we can desire. Amen.

   ❖ You have already been cleansed by the word that I have spoken to you. Abide in me as I abide in you. *John 15:3-4a*

   ● Praise the LORD from the heavens; praise him in the heights. *Psalm 148:1*

✪ *The Lord's Prayer*

✝ Thanks be to God, who gives us victory over death through Jesus our Lord. Amen.

Noon Variation

   ❖ Beloved, let us love one another, because love is from God; everyone who loves is born of God and knows God. *1 John 4:7*

   ● The loving-kindness of the LORD fills the whole earth. *Psalm 33:5b*

Evening Variation

   ❖ Peace I leave with you; my peace I give to you. I do not give to you as the world gives. Do not let your hearts be troubled, and do not let them be afraid. *John 14:27*

   ● May God give us his blessing, and may all the ends of the earth stand in awe of him. *Psalm 67:7*

Ascension Day
(Thursday)

✝ Alleluia! Christ is risen. The Lord is risen indeed. Alleluia!

✿ Almighty God, whose Son Jesus ascended far above all heavens, give us faith to perceive his presence in his church on earth. Amen.

❖ And [Jesus] said to them, "Go into all the world and proclaim the good news to the whole creation. . . ." So then the Lord Jesus . . . was taken up into heaven and sat down at the right hand of God. *Mark 16:15, 19*

● God has gone up with a shout, the LORD with the sound of the ram's-horn. *Psalm 47:5*

✿ *The Lord's Prayer*

✝ Thanks be to God, who gives us victory over death through Jesus our Lord. Amen.

Seventh Week in Easter

Morning Prayer

✝ Alleluia! Christ is risen. The Lord is risen indeed. Alleluia!

✪ O God, King of Glory, you have exalted your only Son Jesus Christ: do not leave us comfortless, but send your Holy Spirit to strengthen us to follow where he leads. Amen.

   ❖ I have made your name known to those whom you gave me from the world. They were yours ... and they have kept your word. *John 17:6*

   ● Blessed be the LORD day by day, the God of our salvation, who bears our burdens. *Psalm 68:19*

✪ *The Lord's Prayer*

✝ Thanks be to God, who gives us victory over death through Jesus our Lord. Amen.

Noon Variation

   ❖ This is the testimony: God gives us eternal life, and this life is in his Son. Whoever has the Son has life. *1 John 5:11-12a*

   ● For the LORD Most High is to be feared; he is the great King over all the earth. *Psalm 47:2*

Evening Variation

   ❖ "Come." ... Let everyone who is thirsty come. Let anyone who wishes take the water of life as a gift. *Revelation 22:17*

   ● The heavens declare his righteousness, and all the peoples see his glory. *Psalm 97:6*

Week Beginning with the Day of Pentecost

Morning Prayer

✝ The Spirit of the Lord fills the whole earth. Let us praise his holy name.

✱ O God, King of Glory, you have exalted your only Son Jesus Christ: do not leave us comfortless, but send your Holy Spirit to strengthen us to follow where he leads. Amen.

❖ Suddenly from heaven there came a sound like the rush of a violent wind, and it filled the entire house. . . . Divided tongues, as of fire, appeared among them. . . . All of them were filled with the Holy Spirit. *Acts 2:2-4*

● You send forth your Spirit, and they are created; and so you renew the face of the earth. *Psalm 104:31*

✱ *The Lord's Prayer*

✝ Thanks be to God, who gives us victory over death through Jesus our Lord. Amen.

Noon Variation

❖ Now there are varieties of gifts, but the same Spirit. . . . To each is given the manifestation of the Spirit for the common good. *1 Corinthians 12:4, 7*

● The LORD looks down from heaven, and beholds all the people in the world. *Psalm 33:13*

Evening Variation

❖ "Peace be with you. As the Father has sent me, so I send you." When he had said this, he breathed on them and said, "Receive the Holy Spirit." *John 20:21-22*

● Indeed, our heart rejoices in him, for in his holy Name we put our trust. *Psalm 33:21*

The Season after Pentecost

• • • • •

A Time of Growing in the Lord

The season after Pentecost is the longest season of the church year, lasting approximately six months. It begins and ends with two special days.

The first Sunday after Pentecost is known as Trinity Sunday. On this day we ponder the mystery of a God who we know in three forms: the Creator, who gives us life; the Savior, who gives his life for us; and the Holy Spirit, who inspires us to live our lives in the power of the Resurrection.

The last Sunday of Pentecost, which always falls between November 20 and November 26, is known as Christ the King Sunday. This is a day on which we remember that Christ, not man, is sovereign. The following Sunday is the first Sunday in Advent.

The Pentecost season is a time to listen to our Lord and to grow in knowledge and understanding. It focuses on living out our faith in Christ as we are led by the Holy Spirit.

Note: Because the date on which we celebrate Easter varies from year to year, the dates on which we celebrate the Day of Pentecost and Trinity Sunday vary as well. Taking these dates into account, choose the set of prayers here that is closest to the week following Trinity Sunday. That may mean that you'll skip a prayer set or two to stay on track with the calendar of the church year.

Week Beginning with Trinity Sunday

Morning Prayer

✝ In the name of the Father, and of the Son, and of the Holy Spirit.

✪ Almighty God, keep us steadfast in faith and worship, and bring us at last to see you in your eternal glory. Amen.

   ❖ Go therefore and make disciples of all nations, baptizing them in the name of the Father and of the Son and of the Holy Spirit, and teaching them to obey everything that I have commanded you. *Matthew 28:19-20a*

   ● Praise [God] for his mighty acts; praise him for his excellent greatness. *Psalm 150:2*

✪ *The Lord's Prayer*

✝ Holy is our Lord God, who was and is and is to come! Amen.

Noon Variation

   ❖ When we cry, "Abba! Father!" it is that very Spirit bearing witness with our spirit that we are children of God. *Romans 8:15b-16*

   ● He has made the whole world so sure that it cannot be moved. *Psalm 93:2*

Evening Variation

   ❖ I heard the voice of the Lord saying, "Whom shall I send, and who will go for us?" And I said, "Here am I; send me!" *Isaiah 6:8*

   ● The LORD shall give strength to his people; the LORD shall give his people the blessing of peace. *Psalm 29:11*

Week of the Sunday Closest to May 25

Morning Prayer

✝ Worship the Lord in the beauty of holiness. Come, let us adore him.

☸ Most loving Father, preserve us from faithless fears and worldly anxieties, that nothing in this life may hide from us the light of love that is immortal in your Son, Jesus Christ. Amen.

  ❖ The LORD has comforted his people, and will have compassion on his suffering ones. *Isaiah 49:13b*

  ● For God alone my soul in silence waits; truly, my hope is in him. *Psalm 62:6*

☸ *The Lord's Prayer*

✝ The glory of the Lord has been revealed, and all flesh shall see it together. Amen.

Noon Variation

  ❖ Consider the lilies of the field, how they grow . . . even Solomon in all his glory was not clothed like one of these. *Matthew 6:28-29*

  ● In God is my safety and my honor; God is my strong rock and my refuge. *Psalm 62:8*

Evening Variation

  ❖ [Those who heed my word are] like a man building a house, who dug deeply and laid the foundation on rock; when a flood arose, the river burst against that house, but could not shake it. *Luke 6:47-48*

  ● Those who are planted in the house of the LORD shall flourish in the courts of our God. *Psalm 92:12*

Week of the Sunday Closest to June 1

Morning Prayer

✝ Worship the Lord in the beauty of holiness. Come, let us adore him.

✪ O God, who sets all things in order both in heaven and earth, put away from us all hurtful things, and give us those things which are profitable for us.

❖ You shall put these words of mine in your heart and soul.... Teach them to your children, talking about them when you are at home and when you are away, when you lie down and when you rise. *Deuteronomy 11:18a, 19*

● Be strong and let your heart take courage, all you who wait for the LORD. *Psalm 31:24*

✪ *The Lord's Prayer*

✝ The grace of our Lord Jesus Christ, and the love of God, and the fellowship of the Holy Spirit be with us all evermore. Amen.

Noon Variation

❖ The sabbath was made for humankind, and not humankind for the sabbath; so the Son of Man is lord even of the sabbath. *Mark 2:27-28*

● Sing with joy to God our strength and raise a loud shout to the God of Jacob. *Psalm 81:1*

Evening Variation

❖ O LORD, God of Israel, there is no God like you in heaven above or on earth beneath, keeping covenant and steadfast love for your servants who walk before you with all their heart. *1 Kings 8:23*

● As for all the gods of the nations, they are but idols; but it is the LORD who made the heavens. *Psalm 96:5*

Week of the Sunday Closest to June 8

Morning Prayer

✝ Worship the Lord in the beauty of holiness. Come, let us adore him.

✪ O God, grant that by your inspiration we may think those things that are right, and by your merciful guiding may do them.

> ❖ Go and learn what this means, "I desire mercy, not sacrifice." For I have come to call not the righteous but sinners. *Matthew 9:13*

> ● Offer to God a sacrifice of thanksgiving and make good your vows to the Most High. *Psalm 50:14*

✪ *The Lord's Prayer*

✝ The grace of our Lord Jesus Christ, and the love of God, and the fellowship of the Holy Spirit be with us all evermore. Amen.

Noon Variation

> ❖ If a kingdom is divided against itself, that kingdom cannot stand. And if a house is divided against itself, that house will not be able to stand. *Mark 3:24-25*

> ● I wait for the LORD; my soul waits for him; in his word is my hope. *Psalm 130:4*

Evening Variation

> ❖ The gospel that was proclaimed by me is not of human origin. . . . I received it through a revelation of Jesus Christ. *Galatians 1:11-12*

> ● Weeping may spend the night, but joy comes in the morning. *Psalm 30:6*

Week of the Sunday Closest to June 15

Morning Prayer

✝ Worship the Lord in the beauty of holiness. Come, let us adore him.

☼ O Lord, keep us in your steadfast faith and love, that we may proclaim your truth with boldness, and minister your justice with compassion. Amen.

❖ The harvest is plentiful, but the laborers are few; therefore ask the Lord of the harvest to send out laborers into his harvest. *Matthew 9:37-38*

● Be joyful in the LORD, all you lands; serve the LORD with gladness and come before his presence with a song. *Psalm 100:1*

☼ *The Lord's Prayer*

✝ The grace of our Lord Jesus Christ, and the love of God, and the fellowship of the Holy Spirit be with us all evermore. Amen.

Noon Variation

❖ The kingdom of God is as if someone would scatter seed on the ground, and would sleep and rise night and day, and the seed would sprout and grow, he does not know how. *Mark 4:26-27*

● The righteous shall flourish like a palm tree, and shall spread abroad like a cedar of Lebanon. *Psalm 92:11*

Evening Variation

❖ We have come to believe in Christ Jesus, so that we might be justified by faith in Christ, and not by doing the works of the law. *Galatians 2:16*

● Happy are they to whom the LORD imputes no guilt, and in whose spirit there is no guile! *Psalm 32:2*

Week of the Sunday Closest to June 22

Morning Prayer

✝ Worship the Lord in the beauty of holiness. Come, let us adore him.

✪ O Lord, help us have perpetual love and reverence for your holy Name, and never fail to help and govern those whom you have set upon the sure foundation of your loving-kindness. Amen.

❖ Just as one man's trespass led to condemnation for all, so one man's act of righteousness leads to justification and life for all. *Romans 5:18*

● Answer me, O LORD, for your love is kind; in your great compassion, turn to me. *Psalm 69:18*

✪ *The Lord's Prayer*

✝ The grace of our Lord Jesus Christ, and the love of God, and the fellowship of the Holy Spirit be with us all evermore. Amen.

Noon Variation

❖ If anyone is in Christ, there is a new creation; everything old has passed away; see, everything has become new! *2 Corinthians 5:17*

● Let them give thanks to the LORD for his mercy and the wonders he does for his children. *Psalm 107:31*

Evening Variation

❖ Those who want to save their life will lose it, and those who lose their life for my sake will save it. *Luke 9:24*

● You have been my helper, and under the shadow of your wings I will rejoice. *Psalm 63:7*

Week of the Sunday Closest to June 29

Morning Prayer

✝ Worship the Lord in the beauty of holiness. Come, let us adore him.

✤ Join us together in unity of spirit with the apostles' teaching, that we may be a holy temple acceptable to you. Amen.

> ❖ We know that Christ, being raised from the dead, will never die again; death no longer has dominion over him. *Romans 6:9*

> ● Truly, the LORD is our ruler; the Holy One of Israel is our King. *Psalm 89:18*

✤ *The Lord's Prayer*

✝ The grace of our Lord Jesus Christ, and the love of God, and the fellowship of the Holy Spirit be with us all evermore. Amen.

Noon Variation

> ❖ You know the generous act of our Lord Jesus Christ, that though he was rich, yet for our sakes he became poor, so that by his poverty you might become rich. *2 Corinthians 8:9*

> ● Light shines in the darkness for the upright; the righteous are merciful and full of compassion. *Psalm 112:4*

Evening Variation

> ❖ The fruit of the Spirit is love, joy, peace, patience, kindness, generosity, faithfulness, gentleness, and self-control. *Galatians 5:22-23a*

> ● O LORD, you are my portion and my cup; it is you who uphold my lot. *Psalm 16:5*

Week of the Sunday Closest to July 6

Morning Prayer

✝ Worship the Lord in the beauty of holiness. Come, let us adore him.

✪ O God, grant us the grace of your Holy Spirit, that we may be devoted to you with our whole heart, and united to one another with pure affection. Amen.

❖ The law of the Spirit of life in Christ Jesus has set you free from the law of sin and of death. *Romans 8:2*

● The LORD is faithful in all his words and merciful in all his deeds. *Psalm 145:14*

✪ *The Lord's Prayer*

✝ The grace of our Lord Jesus Christ, and the love of God, and the fellowship of the Holy Spirit be with us all evermore. Amen.

Noon Variation

❖ [The Lord said,] "My grace is sufficient for you, for power is made perfect in weakness." *2 Corinthians 12:9*

● Our eyes look to the LORD our God, until he show us his mercy. *Psalm 123:3*

Evening Variation

❖ May I never boast of anything except the cross of our Lord Jesus Christ, by which the world has been crucified to me, and I to the world. *Galatians 6:14*

● Come and listen, all you who fear God, and I will tell you what he has done for me. *Psalm 66:14*

Week of the Sunday Closest to July 13

Morning Prayer

✝ Worship the Lord in the beauty of holiness. Come, let us adore him.

✺ Grant that we may know and understand what things we ought to do, and may also have grace and power faithfully to accomplish them. Amen.

> ❖ Everyone who thirsts, come to the waters; and you that have no money, come, buy and eat! *Isaiah 55:1*

> ● You prepare the grain, for so you provide for the earth. *Psalm 65:10*

✺ *The Lord's Prayer*

✝ The grace of our Lord Jesus Christ, and the love of God, and the fellowship of the Holy Spirit be with us all evermore. Amen.

Noon Variation

> ❖ For all who are led by the Spirit of God are children of God. You did not receive a spirit of slavery to fall back into fear, but you have received a spirit of adoption. *Romans 8:14-15*

> ● Awesome things will you show us in your righteousness, O God of our salvation. *Psalm 65:5a*

Evening Variation

> ❖ You shall love the Lord your God with all your heart, and with all your soul, and with all your strength, and with all your mind; and your neighbor as yourself. *Luke 10:27*

> ● [The LORD] guides the humble in doing right and teaches his way to the lowly. *Psalm 25:8*

Week of the Sunday Closest to July 20

Morning Prayer

✝ Worship the Lord in the beauty of holiness. Come, let us adore him.

☉ Almighty God, you know our needs before we ask and our ignorance in asking. Have compassion on our weakness, and mercifully give us those things which for our unworthiness we dare not, and for our blindness we cannot ask. Amen.

❖ I consider that the sufferings of this present time are not worth comparing with the glory about to be revealed to us. For the creation waits with eager longing for the revealing of the children of God. *Romans 8:18-19*

● Turn to me and have mercy upon me; give your strength to your servant. *Psalm 86:16*

☉ *The Lord's Prayer*

✝ The grace of our Lord Jesus Christ, and the love of God, and the fellowship of the Holy Spirit be with us all evermore. Amen.

Noon Variation

❖ [God said,] "I dwell in the high and holy place, and also with those who are contrite and humble in spirit, to revive the spirit of the humble, and to revive the heart of the contrite." *Isaiah 57:15*

● The poor shall eat and be satisfied, and those who seek the LORD shall praise him. *Psalm 22:25*

Evening Variation

❖ God chose to make known how great among the Gentiles are the riches of the glory of this mystery, which is Christ in you. *Colossians 1:27*

● LORD, who may dwell in your tabernacle? ... Whoever leads a blameless life and does what is right. *Psalm 15:1-2*

Week of the Sunday Closest to July 27

Morning Prayer

✝ Worship the Lord in the beauty of holiness. Come, let us adore him.

✪ O God, protector of all who trust in you, give us your mercy to pass through things temporal, that we not lose the things eternal. Amen.

   ❖ The kingdom of heaven is like a merchant in search of fine pearls; on finding one pearl of great value, he went and sold all that he had and bought it. *Matthew 13:45-46*

   ● When your word goes forth it gives light; it gives understanding to the simple. *Psalm 119:130*

✪ *The Lord's Prayer*

✝ The grace of our Lord Jesus Christ, and the love of God, and the fellowship of the Holy Spirit be with us all evermore. Amen.

Noon Variation

   ❖ I . . . beg you to lead a life worthy of the calling to which you have been called, with all humility and gentleness, with patience, bearing with one another in love, making every effort to maintain the unity of the Spirit in the bond of peace. *Ephesians 4:1-3*

   ● Tremble, O earth, at the presence of the LORD, at the presence of the God of Jacob. *Psalm 114:7*

Evening Variation

   ❖ Ask, and it will be given you; search, and you will find; knock, and the door will be opened for you. *Luke 11:9*

   ● Though I walk in the midst of trouble, you keep me safe; . . . your right hand shall save me. *Psalm 138:8*

Week of the Sunday Closest to August 3

Morning Prayer

✝ Worship the Lord in the beauty of holiness. Come, let us adore him.

✪ O Lord, cleanse and defend your Church, and protect and govern it always by your goodness. Amen.

❖ The disciples . . . said, "This is a deserted place, and the hour is now late; send the crowds away so that they may go into the villages and buy food for themselves." *Matthew 14:15*

● He rained down manna upon them to eat and gave them grain from heaven. *Psalm 78:24*

✪ *The Lord's Prayer*

✝ The grace of our Lord Jesus Christ, and the love of God, and the fellowship of the Holy Spirit be with us all evermore. Amen.

Noon Variation

❖ You were taught to put away your former way of life . . . and to clothe yourselves with the new self, created according to the likeness of God. *Ephesians 4:22, 24*

● I will open my mouth in a parable; I will declare the mysteries of ancient times. *Psalm 78:2*

Evening Variation

❖ [Jesus said,] "Take care! Be on your guard against all kinds of greed; for one's life does not consist in the abundance of possessions." *Luke 12:15*

● God will ransom my life; he will snatch me from the grasp of death. *Psalm 49:15*

Week of the Sunday Closest to August 10

Morning Prayer

✝ Worship the Lord in the beauty of holiness. Come, let us adore him.

☉ Lord, grant us the spirit to think and do those things that are right, that we may be enabled to live according to your will. Amen.

❖ So Peter . . . started walking on the water, and came toward Jesus. But when he noticed the strong wind, he . . . [began] to sink. . . . Jesus immediately reached out his hand and caught him. *Matthew 14:29-31*

● The LORD shall give strength to his people; the LORD shall give his people the blessing of peace. *Psalm 29:11*

☉ *The Lord's Prayer*

✝ The grace of our Lord Jesus Christ, and the love of God, and the fellowship of the Holy Spirit be with us all evermore. Amen.

Noon Variation

❖ The LORD your God has led you . . . in the wilderness, in order to humble you, testing you to know what was in your heart. *Deuteronomy 8:2*

● I sought the LORD, and he answered me and delivered me out of all my terror. *Psalm 34:4*

Evening Variation

❖ Faith is the assurance of things hoped for, the conviction of things not seen. *Hebrews 11:1*

● By the word of the LORD were the heavens made, by the breath of his mouth all the heavenly hosts. *Psalm 33:6*

Week of the Sunday Closest to August 17

Morning Prayer

✝ Worship the Lord in the beauty of holiness. Come, let us adore him.

✪ Give us grace to receive thankfully the fruits of Jesus' redeeming work, and to follow daily in his holy steps. Amen.

❖ [Those who love the Lord] — these I will bring to my holy mountain, and make them joyful in my house of prayer. *Isaiah 56:6-7*

● May God be merciful to us and bless us, show us the light of his countenance and come to us. *Psalm 67:1*

✪ *The Lord's Prayer*

✝ The grace of our Lord Jesus Christ, and the love of God, and the fellowship of the Holy Spirit be with us all evermore. Amen.

Noon Variation

❖ [Wisdom calls out,] "Lay aside immaturity, and live, and walk in the way of insight." *Proverbs 9:6*

● Great is our LORD and mighty in power; there is no limit to his wisdom. *Psalm 147:5*

Evening Variation

❖ Therefore, since we are surrounded by so great a cloud of witnesses, . . . let us run with perseverance the race that is set before us. *Hebrews 12:1*

● Arise, O God, and rule the earth, for you shall take all nations for your own. *Psalm 82:8*

Week of the Sunday Closest to August 24

Morning Prayer

✝ The earth is the Lord's for he made it. Come, let us adore him.

☉ Grant, O merciful God, that your Church, being gathered in unity by your Holy Spirit, may show your power among all peoples. Amen.

❖ The LORD will comfort Zion; he . . . will make her wilderness like Eden; . . . joy and gladness will be found in her. *Isaiah 51:3*

● Though the LORD be high, he cares for the lowly; he perceives the haughty from afar. *Psalm 138:7*

☉ *The Lord's Prayer*

✝ The grace of our Lord Jesus Christ, and the love of God, and the fellowship of the Holy Spirit be with us all evermore. Amen.

Noon Variation

❖ Choose this day whom you will serve . . . but as for me and my household, we will serve the LORD. *Joshua 24:15*

● Those who run after other gods shall have their troubles multiplied. *Psalm 16:3*

Evening Variation

❖ People will come from east and west, from north and south, and will eat in the kingdom of God. Indeed, some are last who will be first, and some are first who will be last. *Luke 13:29-30*

● Come now and look upon the works of the LORD, what awesome things he has done on earth. *Psalm 46:9*

Week of the Sunday Closest to August 31

Morning Prayer

✝ The earth is the Lord's for he made it. Come, let us adore him.

❂ Lord of all power and might, graft in our hearts the love of your Name; increase in us true religion and bring forth in us the fruit of good works. Amen.

- ❖ Do not be conformed to this world, but be transformed by the renewing of your minds, so that you may discern what is the will of God — what is good and acceptable and perfect. *Romans 12:2*

- ● I will wash my hands in innocence, O LORD, that I may go in procession round your altar. *Psalm 26:6*

❂ *The Lord's Prayer*

✝ The grace of our Lord Jesus Christ, and the love of God, and the fellowship of the Holy Spirit be with us all evermore. Amen.

Noon Variation

- ❖ Be strong in the Lord and in the strength of his power. Put on the whole armor of God, so that you may be able to stand against the wiles of the devil. *Ephesians 6:10-11*

- ● In his sight the wicked is rejected, but he honors those who fear the LORD. *Psalm 15:4*

Evening Variation

- ❖ Do not neglect to show hospitality to strangers, for by doing that some have entertained angels without knowing it. *Hebrews 13:2*

- ● It is good for them to be generous in lending and to manage their affairs with justice. *Psalm 112:5*

Week of the Sunday Closest to September 7

Morning Prayer

✝ The earth is the Lord's for he made it. Come, let us adore him.

✣ O Lord, let us trust you with all our hearts; for you resist the proud who confide in their own strength, and never forsake those who boast of your mercy. Amen.

    ❖ Live in harmony with one another; do not be haughty, but associate with the lowly; do not claim to be wiser than you are. *Romans 12:16*

    ● Give me understanding, and I shall keep your law; I shall keep it with all my heart. *Psalm 119:34*

✣ *The Lord's Prayer*

✝ The grace of our Lord Jesus Christ, and the love of God, and the fellowship of the Holy Spirit be with us all evermore. Amen.

Noon Variation

    ❖ Every generous act of giving, with every perfect gift, is from above, coming down from the Father of lights. *James 1:17*

    ● Who made heaven and earth, the seas, and all that is in them; who keeps his promise for ever. *Psalm 146:5*

Evening Variation

    ❖ Choose life so that you and your descendants may live, loving the LORD your God, obeying him, and holding fast to him. *Deuteronomy 30:19-20*

    ● Happy are they who have not walked in the counsel of the wicked, nor lingered in the way of sinners. *Psalm 1:1*

Week of the Sunday Closest to September 14

Morning Prayer

✝ The earth is the Lord's for he made it. Come, let us adore him.

✪ O God, because without you we are not able to please you, mercifully grant that your Holy Spirit may in all things direct and rule our hearts. Amen.

❖ For it is written, "As I live, says the Lord, every knee shall bow to me, and every tongue shall give praise to God." So then, each of us will be accountable to God. *Romans 14:11-12*

● For as the heavens are high above the earth, so is his mercy great upon those who fear him. *Psalm 103:11*

✪ *The Lord's Prayer*

✝ The grace of our Lord Jesus Christ, and the love of God, and the fellowship of the Holy Spirit be with us all evermore. Amen.

Noon Variation

❖ Show me your faith apart from your works, and I by my works will show you my faith. *James 2:18b*

● The LORD watches over the innocent; I was brought very low, and he helped me. *Psalm 116:5*

Evening Variation

❖ I tell you, there is joy in the presence of the angels of God over one sinner who repents. *Luke 15:10*

● I shall teach your ways to the wicked, and sinners shall return to you. *Psalm 51:14*

Week of the Sunday Closest to September 21

Morning Prayer

✝ The earth is the Lord's for he made it. Come, let us adore him.

✪ Grant us, Lord, not to be anxious about earthly things, but to love things heavenly; and to hold fast to those that shall endure. Amen.

   ❖ I knew that you are a gracious God and merciful, slow to anger, and abounding in steadfast love, and ready to relent from punishing. *Jonah 4:2b*

   ● You open wide your hand and satisfy the needs of every living creature. *Psalm 145:17*

✪ *The Lord's Prayer*

✝ The grace of our Lord Jesus Christ, and the love of God, and the fellowship of the Holy Spirit be with us all evermore. Amen.

Noon Variation

   ❖ [Jesus said,] "Whoever welcomes one such child in my name welcomes me, and whoever welcomes me welcomes not me but the one who sent me." *Mark 9:37*

   ● Behold, God is my helper; it is the LORD who sustains my life. *Psalm 54:4*

Evening Variation

   ❖ There is one God; there is also one mediator between God and humankind, Christ Jesus, himself human, who gave himself a ransom for all. *1 Timothy 2:5-6a*

   ● When I called, you answered me; you increased my strength within me. *Psalm 138:4*

Week of the Sunday Closest to September 28

Morning Prayer

✝ The earth is the Lord's for he made it. Come, let us adore him.

✤ O God, you declare your almighty power in showing mercy and pity. Grant us your grace, that we may become partakers of your heavenly treasure. Amen.

    ❖ At the name of Jesus every knee should bend, in heaven and on earth and under the earth, and every tongue should confess that Jesus Christ is Lord. *Philippians 2:10-11*

    ● He guides the humble in doing right and teaches his way to the lowly. *Psalm 25:8*

✤ *The Lord's Prayer*

✝ The grace of our Lord Jesus Christ, and the love of God, and the fellowship of the Holy Spirit be with us all evermore. Amen.

Noon Variation

    ❖ Jesus said, ". . . no one who does a deed of power in my name will be able soon afterward to speak evil of me. Whoever is not against us is for us." *Mark 9:39-40*

    ● The testimony of the LORD is sure and gives wisdom to the innocent. *Psalm 19:7b*

Evening Variation

    ❖ As for those who in the present age are rich, command them not to be haughty, or to set their hopes on the uncertainty of riches, but rather on God who richly provides us with everything for our enjoyment. *1 Timothy 6:17*

    ● The LORD sets the prisoners free; the LORD opens the eyes of the blind; the LORD lifts up those who are bowed down. *Psalm 146:7*

Week of the Sunday Closest to October 5

Morning Prayer

✝ The earth is the Lord's for he made it. Come, let us adore him.

✡ Almighty God, you are always more ready to hear than we to pray and to give more than we either desire or deserve. Pour upon us the abundance of your mercy . . . through the merits and mediation of Jesus Christ our Savior. Amen.

    ❖ I press on toward the goal for the prize of the heavenly call of God in Christ Jesus. *Philippians 3:14*

    ● Restore us, O God of hosts; show the light of your countenance, and we shall be saved. *Psalm 80:3*

✡ *The Lord's Prayer*

✝ The grace of our Lord Jesus Christ, and the love of God, and the fellowship of the Holy Spirit be with us all evermore. Amen.

Noon Variation

    ❖ So God created humankind in his image, in the image of God he created them; male and female he created them. *Genesis 1:27*

    ● You have made [man] but little lower than the angels; you adorn him with glory and honor. *Psalm 8:6*

Evening Variation

    ❖ Rekindle the gift of God that is within you through the laying on of my hands; for God did not give us a spirit of cowardice, but rather a spirit of power and of love and of self-discipline. *2 Timothy 1:6-7*

    ● Commit your way to the LORD and put your trust in him, and he will bring it to pass. *Psalm 37:5*

Week of the Sunday Closest to October 12

Morning Prayer

✝ The earth is the Lord's for he made it. Come, let us adore him.

✪ Lord, we pray that your grace may always precede and follow us, and that we may continually be given to good works. Amen.

❖ Go therefore into the main streets, and invite everyone you find to the wedding banquet. *Matthew 22:9*

● Surely your goodness and mercy shall follow me all the days of my life, and I will dwell in the house of the LORD forever. *Psalm 23:6*

✪ *The Lord's Prayer*

✝ The grace of our Lord Jesus Christ, and the love of God, and the fellowship of the Holy Spirit be with us all evermore. Amen.

Noon Variation

❖ Seek good and not evil, that you may live; and so the LORD, the God of hosts, will be with you. *Amos 5:14*

● LORD, you have been our refuge from one generation to another. *Psalm 90:1*

Evening Variation

❖ Do your best to present yourself to God as one approved by him, a worker who has no need to be ashamed, rightly explaining the word of truth. *2 Timothy 2:15*

● The LORD is high above the nations, and his glory above the heavens. *Psalm 113:4*

Week of the Sunday Closest to October 19

Morning Prayer

✝ The earth is the Lord's for he made it. Come, let us adore him.

✿ Almighty God, preserve the works of your mercy, that your Church may persevere with steadfast faith in the confession of your Name. Amen.

   ❖ [Jesus said,] "Give therefore to the emperor the things that are the emperor's, and to God the things that are God's." *Matthew 22:21*

   ● Ascribe to the LORD the honor due his Name; bring offerings and come into his courts. *Psalm 96:8*

✿ *The Lord's Prayer*

✝ The grace of our Lord Jesus Christ, and the love of God, and the fellowship of the Holy Spirit be with us all evermore. Amen.

Noon Variation

   ❖ We do not have a high priest who is unable to sympathize with our weaknesses, but we have one who in every respect has been tested as we are, yet without sin. *Hebrews 4:15*

   ● You are my refuge and my stronghold, my God in whom I put my trust. *Psalm 91:2*

Evening Variation

   ❖ All scripture is inspired by God and is useful for teaching . . . so that everyone who belongs to God may be proficient, equipped for every good work. *2 Timothy 3:16-17*

   ● My help comes from the LORD, the maker of heaven and earth. *Psalm 121:2*

Week of the Sunday Closest to October 26

Morning Prayer

☦ The earth is the Lord's for he made it. Come, let us adore him.

☉ Almighty God, increase in us the gifts of faith, hope, and charity; and, that we may obtain what you promise, make us love what you command. Amen.

> ❖ So deeply do we care for you that we are determined to share with you not only the gospel of God but also our own selves. *1 Thessalonians 2:8*

> ● Show your servants your works and your splendor to their children. *Psalm 90:16*

☉ *The Lord's Prayer*

☦ The grace of our Lord Jesus Christ, and the love of God, and the fellowship of the Holy Spirit be with us all evermore. Amen.

Noon Variation

> ❖ God is not unjust; he will not overlook your work and the love that you showed for his sake in serving the saints. *Hebrews 6:10*

> ● I put my trust in your mercy; my heart is joyful because of your saving help. *Psalm 13:5*

Evening Variation

> ❖ The Lord stood by me and gave me strength, so that through me the message might be fully proclaimed and all the Gentiles might hear it. *2 Timothy 4:17*

> ● No good thing will the LORD withhold from those who walk with integrity. *Psalm 84:11*

Week of the Sunday Closest to November 2

Morning Prayer

✝ The earth is the Lord's for he made it. Come, let us adore him.

✪ Merciful God, it is only by your gift that we offer you true and laudable service. Grant that we may run without stumbling to obtain your heavenly promises. Amen.

❖ We also constantly give thanks to God . . . that when you received the word of God . . . from us, you accepted it not as a human word but as what it really is, God's word, which is also at work in you believers. *1 Thessalonians 2:13*

● Send out your light and your truth, that they may lead me, and bring me to your holy hill and to your dwelling. *Psalm 43:3*

✪ *The Lord's Prayer*

✝ The grace of our Lord Jesus Christ, and the love of God, and the fellowship of the Holy Spirit be with us all evermore. Amen.

Noon Variation

❖ Hear, O Israel: The LORD is our God, the LORD alone. You shall love the LORD your God with all your heart, and with all your soul, and with all your might. *Deuteronomy 6:4-5*

● With my whole heart I seek you; let me not stray from your commandments. *Psalm 119:10*

Evening Variation

❖ [Jesus said,] "Today salvation has come to this house. . . . For the Son of Man came to seek out and to save the lost." *Luke 19:9-10*

● You are my hiding-place; you preserve me from trouble; you surround me with shouts of deliverance. *Psalm 32:8*

Week of the Sunday Closest to November 9

Morning Prayer

✝ The earth is the Lord's for he made it. Come, let us adore him.

✪ O God, whose Son came into the world to make us children of God: Grant that, having this hope, we may purify ourselves and be made like him. Amen.

❖ For the Lord himself . . . will descend from heaven. . . . Then we who are alive . . . will be caught up in the clouds together . . . to meet the Lord in the air; and so we will be with the Lord forever. *1 Thessalonians 4:16-17*

● You are my helper and my deliverer; O LORD, do not tarry. *Psalm 70:6*

✪ *The Lord's Prayer*

✝ The grace of our Lord Jesus Christ, and the love of God, and the fellowship of the Holy Spirit be with us all evermore. Amen.

Noon Variation

❖ A poor widow came and put in two small copper coins. . . . [Jesus said,] "Truly I tell you, this poor widow has put in more than all those. . . . She out of her poverty has put in everything she had, all she had to live on." *Mark 12:42-44*

● The LORD loves the righteous; the LORD cares for the stranger; he sustains the orphan and widow, but frustrates the way of the wicked. *Psalm 146:8*

Evening Variation

❖ I know that my Redeemer lives, and that at the last he will stand upon the earth; and after my skin has been thus destroyed, then in my flesh I shall see God. *Job 19:25-26*

● I call upon you, O God, for you will answer me; incline your ear to me and hear my words. *Psalm 17:6*

Week of the Sunday Closest to November 16

Morning Prayer

✝ The earth is the Lord's for he made it. Come, let us adore him.

✪ Blessed Lord, grant us so to hear holy Scriptures, read, mark, learn, and inwardly digest them, that we may embrace the hope of everlasting life. Amen.

❖ Since we belong to the day, let us be sober, and put on the breastplate of faith and love, and for a helmet the hope of salvation. *1 Thessalonians 5:8*

● LORD, you have been our refuge from one generation to another. *Psalm 90:1*

✪ *The Lord's Prayer*

✝ The grace of our Lord Jesus Christ, and the love of God, and the fellowship of the Holy Spirit be with us all evermore. Amen.

Noon Variation

❖ False messiahs and false prophets will appear and produce signs and omens, to lead astray, if possible, the elect. But be alert; I have already told you everything. *Mark 13:22-23*

● All my delight is upon the godly that are in the land, upon those who are noble among the people. *Psalm 16:2*

Evening Variation

❖ We were not idle when we were with you . . . but with toil and labor we worked night and day, so that we might not burden any of you. *2 Thessalonians 3:7b-8*

● In righteousness shall [God] judge the world and the peoples with equity. *Psalm 98:10*

Christ the King Sunday

Morning Prayer

✝ The earth is the Lord's for he made it. Come, let us adore him.

✪ Almighty God, whose will it is to restore all things in your Son: Mercifully grant that the peoples of the earth may be brought together under his most gracious rule. Amen.

❖ I was hungry and you gave me food, I was thirsty and you gave me something to drink, I was a stranger and you welcomed me. *Matthew 25:35*

● Come, let us bow down, and bend the knee, and kneel before the LORD our Maker. *Psalm 95:6*

✪ *The Lord's Prayer*

✝ The grace of our Lord Jesus Christ, and the love of God, and the fellowship of the Holy Spirit be with us all evermore. Amen.

Noon Variation

❖ "I am the Alpha and Omega," says the Lord God, who is and who was and who is to come, the Almighty. *Revelation 1:8*

● Ever since the world began, your throne has been established; you are from everlasting. *Psalm 93:3*

Evening Variation

❖ I myself will gather the remnant of my flock . . . and I will bring them back to their fold, and they shall be fruitful and multiply. *Jeremiah 23:3*

● Come now and look upon the works of the LORD, what awesome things he has done on earth. *Psalm 46:9*

Additional Sources and Materials

More information and other prayers for the Anglican prayer beads can be found in these volumes:

The Anglican Rosary by Lynn C. Bauman, published by Praxis, Route 1, Box 190-B, Telephone, TX 75488.

Holding Your Prayers in Your Hands by Kristin M. Elliott and Betty Kay Seibt, published by Open Hands, 624 West University Drive, Suite 110, Denton, TX 76201.

Below are several useful Web sites for ordering beads and for finding additional prayers for Anglican rosaries, Anglican prayer beads, and Christian prayer beads:

http://www.gigibeads.net/prayerbeads/prayers/prayers1.html

http://www.solitariesofdekoven.org/Prayer_beads.html

http://www.episcopalbookstore.com

http://www.cathedralrosaries.com/index.php

http://www.kingofpeace.org/prayerbeads.htm

http://www.spiritofprayer.net/